GW00601002

ANCHOR
BOOKS

RHYME AND REASON

Edited by

Rachael Radford

First published in Great Britain in 2003 by
ANCHOR BOOKS
Remus House,
Coltsfoot Drive,
Peterborough, PE2 9JX
Telephone (01733) 898102

HB ISBN 1 84418 104 9
SB ISBN 1 84418 105 7

FOREWORD

Anchor Books is a small press, established in 1992, with the aim of promoting readable poetry to as wide an audience as possible.

We hope to establish an outlet for writers of poetry who may have struggled to see their work in print.

The poems presented here have been selected from many entries, and as always editing proved to be a difficult task.

I trust this selection will delight and please the authors and all those who enjoy reading poetry.

Rachael Radford
Editor

CONTENTS

COMMUNITY WOES

I tried and tried to start a community,
But alas it was in vain,
I tried and tried to bring people together,
But they would not board the train.

2befriends.com is what I had in mind,
But they did not want to know.
How then could I build a community,
When they would not even show?

I tried and tried to start a community,
I thought it would be fine.
I'd spent the money and the hours,
But they wouldn't give me their time.

I'll not give up, it means a lot,
Why you just wait and see.
I'm sure it's just a matter of time,
For this on-line community.

Lee Delmont

MY FEELINGS

I think this world is going to pot,
Running the country, they don't give a jot.
Gain and fame seems to mean the most
Of this, to one and all calmly boast.

Sadly they have no time for others,
Always in a hurry so don't bother.
A cheerful smile a sweet hello,
Doesn't cost a thing to show.

Years ago a friendly chat, a loving smile,
Would make you happy for a while.
Communities today are like strangers,
Can't trust each other so cause danger.

Evelyn M Harding

TIME CHANGE

Community, a word reappearing from days in the past.
The parochial outlook, of many isolated groups,
has little meaning, to this new wider race,
as does their ideals, now slowing in faltering pace

Self and possession have now taken over,
Couldn't care less, it's not my concern.
We must have profit, to many is all that matters,
now called progress, leaving countless lives in tatters.

Yet those who do care, trying to revive what was good,
are accused of living in the past, as dreamers do.
A world now intent on self indulgent destruction,
heeds not the call for community reconstruction.

Hatred and crime in all its forms, is now a part of life.
Blame anyone available, for community failures.
Truth the elusive factor is difficult to find,
true to oneself, comes from your own soul and mind.

To those so inclined in rebuilding community spirit,
be aware, the enormous task, brings little reward.
Even friends, admirers now most sceptical to believe,
may not join and follow, but keep on with faith, to achieve.

Maurice Wilkinson

TEDDY BEARS, FROGS AND PIGS

This ode is written to celebrate
Teddy bears, frogs and pigs for Relate!
They came with their owners for afternoon tea
At the Tettenhall home of John the B:
The sun did shine for this fund-raising do
With white elephant stand, tombola too;
And guests poured in (no Sunday slumbers),
How lovely! Relate staff were there in numbers!
Earl Grey was there in teabag form
And Bob the Builder in uniform:
A bear from Beatties sat there as a sentry
As Cyril from Telford took money for entry:
Margaret did teas or orange or cola,
And Jan was superb setting up the tombola!
It all went so well, lots of money was spent
It was fun as we sought Relate funds to augment.
What more can I say? Well, great joy abounds,
For we raised for Relate a full three hundred pounds!
Let's celebrate now with wild dances and jigs,
And thanks be to teddy bears, frogs and pigs!

John Birkett

COMMUNITIES THROUGH LIFE

There's a great many different communities
All very different indeed:
Your babyhood - with your parents, seeing to every need.
People gather round, to fuss and to admire
Baby laps it up - what more could she desire?

Nursery school, first time without one's mummy near
Some adore the company: others have little fear.
All the days of schoolhood: the nervous first-job days,
But as to outdoor activities, you can choose in many ways.

Now you're in a community of people with same views
In your clubs and societies, with similar hobbies you choose.
Sport: writing: painting: acting: photography, maybe,
Comparing your successes and failures - great variety!

Eventually, you're getting on and want some quieter ways
You enter a pleasant rest home, with friends of similar age.
You can still have quieter hobbies - writing tales or simple rhyme,
You're in your last community and still have a pleasant time.

Marjorie Cowan

TOGETHERNESS

Community means togetherness
Or folk in the same locality,
Those who share accommodation
Now what does it mean to me?
Well . . . it means solidarity
People having a common cause,
All pulling together and helping
These used to be unwritten laws.
As a child I lived in a tenement
Where folk were friendly to everyone,
All shared their trials and traumas
And together they had lots of fun.
During the war and in times of trouble
Being a neighbour meant being a friend,
They delivered each other's babies
In time of death . . . they helped out at the end.
No one dreamt of locking their doors
Mind you then we were able to trust
Children were reared to show respect
And poor folk would share their last crust.
Nowadays, however, things are so different
Folk lock their doors and often live in fear
As children run riot and out of control
And youths attack anyone who is near.
People are scared to help one another
Or go out in their cars alone at night
I feel we've lost the sense of community
It would take a miracle to make things come right.

Mary Anne Scott

HEARTFELT MEMORIES

It was just twenty days from Christmas in nineteen ninety-two
When first we spied the home that we were moving to.
A smile and a wave from across the road, told us a friend was near,
And Inverness Close welcomed us with neighbourly Christmas cheer.

Kind friends had names: greetings exchanged and stories told,
Christmas bells rang out - no snow nor icy cold.
A card was delivered to our door - a Christmas card you see,
Our dear, dear neighbour greeted us, and a real good friend was she.

Weeks sped by - we soon settled in
A bit impatient, our garden to trim.
Bulbs and plants we set and grew,
In good time we had, this wonderful view.

Our lawns are now lush, multicoloured flowers abound
Our home is our haven, with our treasures all around.
We greet you all, with ten thousand thanks,
Neighbours, family and friends, esteemed high in rank.

Kathleen Aldridge

TEACHER TRAINING DAY

Teacher training day - pupil's rest day,
a welcome break, for both,
the pupils can have a lie in, snug in their beds,
under their duvets, pulled high, over their heads,
or whatever else instead,

while their teachers are busy working away,
at school, planning ahead,
for them,
for tomorrow,
and the days to follow;

and at the end of the day,
the teachers go home,
happy and relaxed,
with the feeling of well being,
after their day,
free from cheek, insults and all that they take,
and most importantly,
without a headache.

Jane Milthorp

AMALFI

The warm sun welcomes you with open arms,
The glittering turquoise sea beguiles you with its charms
The bustling, chattering people walk quickly in their stride,
But have the time to say, 'Bon Giorno', with smiles they cannot hide.
You sit down in a restaurant, and given time to settle down,
To watch the sea, now turned dark blue, while the sun sets like a crown.
Far out on the horizon white ships sail serenely by,
Homing into the marina, to anchor and to lie
Up for the night, and then to stroll the brightly lit promenade,
Happy to be in Amalfi, and to hear the musician's serenade.
The mountains above Amalfi are covered in trees and bright flowers,
And walking up there is pure delight, climbing age old steps for hours.
The welcome from Neapolitan's, will certainly warm your heart,
They have their own outlook on life, which definitely sets them apart.
And for those of us who've been lucky enough to share,
                                    if only for a while,
A way of life so full of warmth, that just remembering
                                    makes you smile.

Eileen Cuddy Buckley

COMMUNITY SPIRIT

What drives the human soul to share
in life and death, in common care?
What instinct puts another first,
and hearts with fellow-feeling burst?

We seek life in community
with humankind for family.
From mother's love and father's care
we learn with others how to share.

Most loving species on the Earth
'Sapiens' has collective worth.
In common weal and sympathy,
a uniting needful empathy.

Spurning all solidarity
Some seek libertine anarchy.
Entering a more selfish plea
to ask - 'What's in it just for me?'

Happiness, in experience,
May not be found in such a stance.
Support for others improves life,
Aggression simply leads to strife.

From early times, before the Flood,
The human race shares in one blood
Thicker than water, so 'tis said,
Spirit sustained by living bread.

Brotherhood shared in unity
Sisterhood real in equity
One world is our best charted course
One Father, the uniting force.

Jo Allen

HOMECOMING

Paint me with people, with kinfolk all thronging,
Drop me on doorsteps, start bells all ding-donging.
Be sorry I went, hope you missed me with longing,
'Cause here rests my heart in the nest of belonging.

Hoist up flapping flags to hurrah me home
Treat toasts and down drinks that sparkle and foam.
Dance in the market and sing in the hall
A linking of arms and welcomes from all.

Black years of my wanders in regions unkind
This is the welcome that fuelled my mind.
Hope travelled with dreams of which this is one,
Oh pray it may pass for a prodigal son.

Sarah Blackmore

THROUGH OTHERS' EYES

'Aren't human beings difficult?'
A man once said to me,
But I wonder just how difficult that man was
To others, who see as he can't see.

'Mum's in one of her moods today,'
A disgruntled miss exclaimed,
But I wonder how much tolerance was flowing,
To make that young miss feel so free from blame.

It's one thing to be self assured
When tackling daily life,
But I wonder if folk realise how pleasant,
To smooth a path, instead of causing strife.

I just know this, life's better now,
I'm older, wise to see,
But I wonder, am I wise enough to see
Myself, as clear as other people see?

Joan Hammond

GROWING WISE (WITH AGE)

Judge not a man by what he wears
His worldly wealth or how he fares
Nor by the money he may make
A better way - a man's handshake.
The truth with words a man may hide
Though deeds well done can't be denied
And in the look that's in the eyes
There lies the truth one can't disguise.

Cecil Lewis

ADVICE

Why will you not listen
When you are given advice?
Why will you keep continuing
The destruction of your life?

Why must you keep on taking drugs
That will destroy you in the end?
Why must you hurt your family
Even drive them 'around the bend.'

They do their best to help you
To give you a better interest
Why must you keep ignoring
When they've given of their best?

My advice to you, is to take stock
Remember the person you were
Get some help, see some sense
Make life much easier to bear!

Constance Chant

THRIFT

If floral thrift can enhance a few carnations,
To be thrifty in life can ease situations,
We like the best that money can buy,
While the best we can afford would often suffice.

To live within our income day after day,
Tests our willpower, sounds boring and limits our play,
To balance our lives and balance our budget,
Is never easy but it is possible to do it.

When we over spend we are no longer solvent,
Were we carried away on the spur of the moment?
When we stop to think and count the cost,
We realise the pleasure has gone into our loss.

It is never too late to let thrift have a say,
As we plan and prepare to pay our way,
Then to save, spend, or juggle with what is left,
Means we now know the way to pass the test.

Kathleen McBurney

COMMUNITY SPIRIT WAS WHAT WE HAD

There was one thing you could depend
Community spirit was what we had
Down near the docks in the East End.

Our fathers worked hard and played fast
Community spirit was what we had
Friendship and relationships where made to last.

When someone died Mrs Burke laid them out
Community spirit was what we had
And all for a nice cold bottle of stout.

When someone got married we all took the food
Community spirit was what we had
No one took notice of the jokes that were crude.

We queued up for the jumble sales, second hand for us.
Community spirit was what we had
Did not have cars, we walked or got the bus.

Us old uns we remember the hard times
Community spirit was what we had
It's different times now, far worse crimes.

Moira Jean Clelland

ROSIE

Rosie felt so very smart,
As she sat beneath the tree,
Her heart was thumping loudly
As she bent to rub her knee.
I think I did a grand old job
I ran as fast as ever,
It might have been a different tale
If it wasn't for the weather.
The sun shone bright and sparkly
I'm glad it didn't rain
I might have slipped and fallen down
And maybe caught again.
She heard the dogs all barking
They sounded very near,
Her ear pricked up, her eyes alight
Feeling cold with fear.
I'll have to get a move on,
And find a safer place,
Try to cover up my tracks
So they won't leave a trace.
Something snarled beside her
And she turned to look around,
But before she chanced to make a move
It pulled her to the ground.
Rosie didn't make it,
Was torn from limb to limb.
Although she'd tried so very hard
Her fate had stepped right in.

Susan Stark

NEW ERA HONOURS

The mayor was in a state of shock,
whatever should he do?
Someone had lost the mayoral chain
and royalty was due.

They had searched among the archives
and almost everywhere -
even 'phoned the local pawnshop
to ask if it was there.

For help, the mayor looked to the clerk,
whatever could be done?
Though he was also in the dark,
he had a bright, young son.

'It's very simple,' said the lad,
'with tinfoil and some glue,
I'll make a chain of paper clips
and that will see you through.'

So that's exactly what he did
and everything was fine.
When the council was presented,
the boy was first in line.

Sometime later, to the palace
the mayor went for his gong,
and the queen said to his worship,
'Did you bring the boy along?

We never really thanked him for
his economic tip.
Instead of handing medals out,
it's now a paper clip!'

Ron Dean

HOME PATCH

Communities work best,
When problems arise,
Because they all work together to the same end.
Neighbour helps neighbour putting everything at one side.
National events,
Working parties formed,
All joined together and give their support.

Community workings all done with pride,
From old people's homes, Boy Scouts and
Girl Guides, Rotary and Lions clubs all
Doing their bit.

The inbloomers creating utopia it seems.
Religious buildings standing there providing for people's needs,
Elected members standing their ground
Trying to please all they can.

G F Snook

THE BELVEDERE BOYS

In a quiet Surrey village
Live a band of gallant men,
They have mostly all spent out their days at sea.
But now they come to stay,
From those lands so far away,
For a bit of 'terrafirma' in the autumn of their days.

They are all tried and true.
These generous men in blue,
They're the Boys of Belvedere.

There is songbird Dave, whose ringing tones
Could make him a local star,
And cheery George who plays the spoons,
When we gather for a singsong in the bar.

Why we've never seen such cheer,
As we have seen over here -
With the Boys of Belvedere - bless their hearts!

Stamp your feet, clap your hands,
Give a whistle, give a cheer,
For the Boys, for the Boys,
For the Boys of Belvedere!

M Fitzpatrick-Jones

THE WONDERFUL GIFTS THAT I HAVE

God gave me a body, and so many gifts does it hold
I have a mind that learns through life on what it's told.
There are my brown eyes, for wonderful things to see
that will hold so many precious moments, just for me.
A funny shaped nose to smell a beautiful scented rose
it sneezes, attishoo! into a dainty hanky one blows.
Using my mouth to take food and drink, so refreshing
and to make sounds and words that are so expressing.
At each side of my head, ears to listen to every sound
people talking, birds singing, music playing all around.
Two arms, a pair of hands for a dear loved one to behold
legs and feet to run, walk and play, and to be very bold.
At its centre a warm heart beats to give it life each day
I cherish these great gifts and to thank my God I pray.

B M Attwood

THE PARK AT PLAY

Traffic sails - zoomingly by
while only a few hundred
grassy yards away,
all are blindly oblivious
consumed in play.

Juveniles wreak havoc
as teens meet and court,
while yet others
partake in sport,
and all the while
workers distracted by naught.

Dogs chasing sticks
toddlers take advantage
as in dirt they mix,
social strollers meander
frolicking couples at tricks.

Amazed by it all
elderly watch,
talk and sit,
this once was theirs
in bygone days
to enjoy and flit.

Contrasting lifestyles
yet intermixed,
as time flies onward
till twilight's fixed.

Gary J Finlay

DAY OF DECISION

Two went walking down the street together.
Umbrellas spread wide against wet weather.

It required resolve to stay on their feet.
Even so they were half blown down the street.

'My brolly's turned inside out,' one muttered.
'S-sorry. Wind. Can't hear!' - answer stuttered.

The second umbrellas was plucked away
as someone's dustbin came rolling their way.

'That brolly's broken!' she then discovered,
'and that means my hairstyle's left uncovered!'

To escape rain and bin they sought shelter;
through puddles they skidded helter-skelter.

Yet car wheels ensured an extra soaking.
'We're not ducks or frogs!' he said, voice croaking.

'But how are we to survive this weather?
Here dodging drops, we despair together!'

Oddly, the day each was saturated
was the one their future was decided.

Extra-strong umbrellas they would design.
Profits with their savings they would combine.

Brollies showing ducks followed by their brood.
Frogs leaping . . . brollies to suit any mood.

With so much rain splashing down from the sky
a houseboat their ideal home to buy.

Chris Creedon

LIFE LESSON

I started off in this world
Thinking it was good
I guess it was the way
That I thought it should.

I never knew then
That it could be this bad
Left as a baby
Without a dad.

As a young boy
I tried to grow
But people didn't see
They didn't want to know.

All they did was laugh
And make fun of me
They didn't seem to care about
The feelings inside of me.

I tried to get through this
To a teenager
Still it remained
Judged by my cover.

I fell in love
With my best friend
But she's gone
Now I'll never love again.

Now you tell me
How to stop this pain
Without a gun or blade
Straight to my brain.

So in life
If there's one thing I've learnt
Care about yourself
You'll never get burnt.

Simon McAlear

CRAZY MAY

'I believe in buying shoes that will last,' said May.
'So I bought a pair the wrong size today
Then I won't you see
Wear them,' said she.
'That way they will last forever I say!'

Joan Wylde

WHAT DO WE NEED?

There's quite a difference between men and women
Their needs are not the same,
One thing they do both have in common
Is the fact that with age they change.

When young, healthy youth are strong and keen,
The urge is there to breed,
Nature has a particular way of
planting fertile seeds.

The mother (human, animal and soil)
receives and tends the prize.
They grow in water and in warmth,
nurtured until they rise.

The father helps and then protects
his tiny prodigy.
He likes to feel and live in style
Comfort is his main need.

A woman's needs are not the same.
She likes security,
and love when it is shown to her -
not force, she must be free.

The young grow up and move away,
They break the cord and go,
but the old ones left must carry on
in the only way they know.

They cannot change from what they are,
they want familiar things,
but in their hearts they know they've lost,
there's nothing left but strings.

Doris E Pullen

OPEN TO THE BONE

She said that we'd been chosen,
Though I did not know her well,
But her body seemed to bind me,
Where her silk and satin fell.

She let me read her diary,
So I let her read my mind,
And we looked down on our bodies,
Where our hands and hearts entwined.

Her timeless eyes burned brightly,
But they did not burn for me,
So I asked the stars to tell me,
The ending to my story.

But the vision that they showed me,
Was older than the night,
So I threw down all my armour,
For I had no will to fight.

Yes, she'll open up her gardens,
When she knows you have to see,
And you pay the price forever,
Though she swears the journey's free.

The fires will leave her body,
When you run to claim your prize,
And you'll curse the dying embers,
As she fades before your eyes.

One day you're sure to meet her,
So I'll give you some advice,
Don't let her fires burn you,
For the flames are cold as ice.

And you who think you know me;
Well you did not know me then,
But pain must herald wisdom,
To make us better men.

Kevin Hodge

WISDOM

I've always longed for wisdom,
From teenage years long gone;
To say to those much younger,
That way just might be wrong.

It always gave good feelings
To know that I was right,
But not the time to speak it,
My tongue I'd have to bite.

But wisdom comes as years pass,
Not just the rights and wrongs;
But knowing how, when and where
To kerb, the love that longs.

Wisdom comes but pain comes too,
To know but not advise;
To have to see those young ones
Be hurt and cut to size.

There is no point in saying,
'You know, I told you so,'
Just be there to hold their hand,
Your wisdom then they'll know.

Janet Bowen

REALITY

Reality is hard to face
The dream is dead and gone to waste.
An illusion's flown - a world apart
The truth has borne a broken heart.

The dreamer's price is high to pay
For image unreal and far away
From life's hard core and rude awakening,
Now reality . . . silently waiting.

Margaret Bernard

AGE

As we grow old we also grow wise
We learn how to tell the truth from the lies
We learn from our mistakes and try to prevent more
We try to grow rich and abide by the law
Life can be hard but can also be fun
From working all hours to holidays in the sun
We watch with pride as our children grow tall
Yet we yearn for the days when they were still small
We carry on learning as we grow older
With our increase in age our courage gets bolder
We can see the opportunities that abound
And have more respect for the people around
Age is not something that should frighten
Instead we should use it to enlighten.

Marie Westley

BULLIED (2001)

I stood in the playground and watched the line
They were singing and dancing, the name was mine.
They laughed and they jeered, I was only ten
Then they shouted and hit me and laughed again.
I cried inside, I died inside.

Alone in the playground I watched the line
They charged and bellowed, the name was mine
'Old fatty Faulkner' was what I heard
No one would help me, I said not a word but
I cried inside, I died inside.

At the age of eleven, another school
'A little more subtle' the bullying rule.
Nobody knew except them, and me
And it's only now that I can feel free from
The crying inside and the dying inside.

Elizabeth Williams

SEPTEMBER SPECTRE

The fiery late September sun beats down on hard baked clay
Sunbeams dance kissing crisp curls of Dollie fleet footing on her way
Occasional twittering birdsong, blends with chattering voices shrill
Nimble fingered folk pick hops 'I've made it' breathless Dollie cries
speeding down the hill,
'The doctor's calling, Jackie's ill, we think it might be croup,'
The gossip stops and silence falls among the busy group
'Tell both the boys to stay with me when out of school at four,'
'The master's entertaining send them round to the back door.'
Sunlight transforms creeper clad walls to richest ruby hue
The dark forbidding moat now briefly bathed in sapphire blue
While deeply mullioned windows peep like stars so diamond bright
But look! black Jasper's bark announce the boys are now in sight
'We're really hungry Doll' they cry 'What have you cooked to eat?'
Bubble and squeak spits in the pan, 'I've made your favourite treat,'
The supper over 'Now out to play with bat and ball you two.'
Gambolling around with Jasper as if released from distant zoo
'It's time for bed, now not a word creep up back stairs in stockinged
feet.'
'I'll join you when I've washed the plates just snuggle down between
the sheets.'
The bedsteads dance in candlelight illumined by silver moon
'I can't sleep here' poor Archie wails, 'this is the haunted room,'
Jasper must lie on counterpane protecting us and ghosts to catch
Some coloured rag and length of string secures the wooden latch
The clock strikes twelve, a vixen howls the door latch clicks or is
the moonlight playing tricks.'
A hooded monk with flickering lamp glides silently across the room
High hackles rise on Jasper's back bright eyes shine scarlet in the gloom
Doll stuffs a sheet between clenched lips 'Go back to sleep, it's just a
dream,'
Morning's here - the cockerel crows bright sunbeams gleam
transfiguring scene

But look! What is that near the cellar door? The spectre's lamp lies on the floor.
'Who left that lamp? It wasn't there last night' the boys declare
'Brave Jasper deserves crisp bacon rind, there must be some to spare.'

Linda Core

LAMENT FOR WEST SMETHWICK PARK

Those dammed city planners have taken away my youth,
on a journey to recall my early days my eyes now see the truth.
West Smethwick Park in the 30s was a place of adventure thrills,
with natural springs, and waterbeds, and undulating hills.

Those damned town hall planners have stolen part of my life,
with flattened plain, and stinking pool, nature in turmoil and strife.
The rubbish tipped, the epitaph, and fish no longer rule. In the name
of progress they call it, uplifting environment scene, but their brains
never function in daylight, and eyes wide open, not see, their own
child's children will never, have within their own tiny grasp,
the beauty, free and God given, that was mine in days now past.

The lilypond has gone, laid bare, and frogs no longer call or share, with
golden fish in that pure clear state. Make way for this thing called
concrete. Flowers beneath a leafy glade, destroyed, dug up with fork
and spade. Natural springs, and watercress beds, and cowslip nodded
their yellow head. Quench your thirst from the staff of life, this indeed
was my paradise.

Falcon, owl, badger and fox, my parents knew all of these spots.
Grandfather Smith hailed from Douglas Road, and more than twice did
stock the lake, with sons, Joe, Jack and Albert showed how to see with
hand and mind the life that's present in tree and grass, and death's no
fear as it comes to pass,
except
from dead dark reeking lake, who dares come now, to partake?

Those dammed city planners, jockeying for job and more pay, can't you
see what you've done to the beauty even though it's late in the day.
Who cast their vote for the idiot, who wantonly goes and destroys, the
area and place of my childhood. The park where we once played as
boys.

Brian V Smith

MY STORY'S IN YOUR GIFT

One day there'll be a story
of the life that I have lived;
I'll be the one who made it,
you'll decide if it's a gift

I have passion for what's possible
and dreams that take me there;
where mountain tops evaporate
in destiny's thin air.

I'll be the story maker,
you'll choose the words for me;
my heart will beat forever
if your voice sets mine free.

I have passion for what's possible
and dreams that take me there;
where mountain tops evaporate
in destiny's thin air.

The story that you tell one day
will be the one I lived;
my life in words you gave me,
my story's in your gift.

I have passion for what's possible
and dreams that take me there;
where mountain tops evaporate
in destiny's thin air.

Tim Coburn

RETIREMENT

We don't sit back in a leisurely way,
But enjoy what we do in every way
We don't have to watch the clock on the wall
And what we do, has no deadline at all.

You don't have to do everything, just today
There is always tomorrow, as some people say
The only prayer is that you can keep your health
Just hope for happiness, not money or wealth.

Take one day at a time, and face life with a smile
Retirement can be such an enjoyable time
Fishing, walking and grandchildren too,
You don't get bored, always plenty to do.

Just thank God to reach this wonderful age
And like a book you are nearing the last page
Take life as it comes, take one day at a time
And be thankful for life yours and mine.

Audrey Haggerty

TOMORROW REPLACES TODAY

Be thankful for today,
Enjoy this given time,
Improving on all done yesterday,
So weave our life's design.

Letting all colours blend and mingle,
Within love every achievement seen,
Grasping opportunities which may arise,
So nothing is a might have been.

Work all things out through logic,
Not guessing or just presume,
Never end a day with discord,
Keep the rhyme going and in tune.

So the day closes tidy as the mind,
No loose strands along the way,
For the pattern of today now woven,
Threads ready for tomorrow - which replaces today.

Brenda Douglass

PLEASE SEND MY ACCOUNT!

Dear Mr Smith,

Your letter to me of April the seventh
has translated me to my seventh heaven!
Your enclosure from the Inspector of Taxes -
a model of brevity and too, ataraxy
brings news of joy and gladness of spirit
that's been my lot, since revelling in it!
What more to say than thank you awfully
for dealing so well with matters lawfully
and bringing about such a state of affairs
as to engender a belief that I'm walking on air!
Thank you again from my hedonist's den
where lassitude compels me to lay down my pen.
But that will be easy to quickly surmount
upon hearing from you with your modest account.
Believe me, dear sir, your considerable achievement
has removed from my shoulders a weight like a bereavement.
There's little to say now that I can foresee
so I'll close this wee note - the rest's o'er to thee.

Bidding you thanks most copiously,
Your sincerest of friends,
I am.

Andrew A Duncan

MY SPECIAL PLACE

There is a place I go to,
Whenever I feel sad,
To evoke old memories,
Then nothing seems so bad!

I look around, remembering,
How things, once used to be,
How it felt, to be, so loved,
When you, were here, with me.

I can feel your arms enfold me,
And troubles, melt away,
Those hypnotic eyes - smile again,
And I'm back to yesterday!

Never was, there need, for words,
We knew each other's thought,
Just to be together, enough
To make life seem, less fraught.

No one knows my secret place,
Unless, my thoughts, they've read,
For where I go for solace now,
Is - just inside my head!

E M Eagle

ANOTHER DAY AT THE FACTORY

In the back of my head, the alarm is ringing,
like somebody playing, loud opera singing.
Best get up now, or I'll be late for work,
I don't want my workmates, saying 'I shirk.'

I arrive there quite early, don't want to be late,
to be called a skiver, now that, I would hate.
I go to the time clock and slot in my card,
knowing the day, is going to be hard.

The Shop Steward, he shouts 'There's a meeting today,'
'We're going to discuss how to get higher pay.'
I go and I listen to what he does say,
We'll go out on strike; There's no other way.

In the back of my mind, I feel something's corrupt,
when I think of the business, that we will disrupt.
I have to go along with them, or get filled with shame,
but I often do wonder, how many feel the same.

I'll be out of this factory, hopefully one day,
before I end up on another strike pay.
All that I want, is to earn honest pay,
so I can afford, to settle down one day.

Meanwhile it's back to the 'production lines',
where machinery hisses, rumbles and whines,
I operate the levers in my usual way,
in the job that I do, day after day.

It's so very boring, watching parts go past,
making sure that all, are going to last.
I should really be grateful for my little role,
working in this factory, as quality control.

Steve Elson

GREY DAYS

A poet might admire the ways
I measure out my hollow days;
With nothing quite so grand as spoons
Or artists talk in living rooms;
No mornings spent on toast and tea,
Or afternoons with friends to see.
My marmalade grows spots of mould
And as I count them, I grow old.

Too late now to try to change,
To alter, digress, rearrange.
I'd love to spit the butt-ends out,
Wrap on a shawl and strut and shout
And after ices, tea and cake,
Sit down with friends and talk of Blake
But lighting up, I pour the wine -
Two other measures of my time.

I watch each smoke ring split apart
And wonder if I have the heart
To put on make-up with creased fingers,
Wipe the dust from where it lingers,
Make a visit, face the street,
Find a lonely man to meet
And just when I believe I dare,
I comb my silvered strands of hair.

I will not come back from the dead,
To say those things still left unsaid.
I would not say I am afraid -
I do not weep, I have not prayed.
My ashtray forms a half-smoked vision
Of chances lost through indecision.
I did not mean for this to be -
I wonder what became of me?

Andrea K Ellis

THE L DRIVER

I've been an L of a driver
Tried to pass my test for a number of years
And just as the great Mr Churchill said
There's been plenty of blood, sweat and tears
At last I got rid of my L plates
Which I did with a great deal of pride
Now instead of my husband being chauffeur
I can take him instead for a ride.

Kathleen Fox-Watson

THE BANK

I went to the bank today,
and paid - in my misery.
I'm saving for a rainy day.
Whenever that might be.
They pay good interest,
of hollow words and tears.
And I have quite a balance,
in an account I've had for years.

The painted lady at the desk
takes hurting hearts on deposit.
So I gladly hand her mine
and feel much better for it.
Then the man behind me, in the line,
starts singing the Honky Tonk blues,
and when he motions me to join,
well, how could I refuse?

I know his lonesome song,
so we sing a verse or two,
and I gain more misery,
before our duet is through.
It's easy to save this way.
The balance builds itself.
And my life is rich and full,
while I'm drowning in my wealth.

M M Graham

MY FAULTS

My husband listed my
faults one night.
What's so bad is
they're all so right!

One: My feelings go too deep,
where another human could
never peep.

Two: I leave the loo door
open wide,
so everyone can see inside.

Three: I put my animals and
birds first in my time,
so everybody else has to
wait in line.

Four: My joy and love of
nature, people, and life
makes me an over-energetic
housewife.

Five: I go to bed in the
early morn, but am awake
listening to the birds at
the crack of dawn.

Six: Living with me is like
heaven or hell,
only my long suffering
husband can tell.

Patricia Gray

REDEVELOPING PROGRESS?

There was a community called Tiger Bay
Where people from all nations came to work, live and play.
To some it was renowned as the dark side of town
Ladies of the night, pubs, brawls, fights.
But to those whose faces did not fit, up in the city.
It was a refuge, from the hatred and the pity.
Simply a place to live where your neighbour was your brother
And it didn't matter his race or creed or colour.
Everyone helped each other.

There was a community called Tiger Bay
And they could really teach us how to work, and live and play.
In harmony, in peace, without instant judgements
Based on prejudice.
But the ships have gone, the docks closed down
And now it's the new and gleaming - 'yuppie' end of town.
Expensive flats far out of reach of the pockets of the locals,
And it's preached that this is regeneration,
Redevelopment - a brighter better future, but for whom?

The new Cardiff Bay - the most exciting place to be
But where's its soul, where's its meaning?
All glitzy restaurants, smart wine bars
Fancy tables, fancy lights hanging from the ceiling.
It makes me sad to see
The end of Tiger Bay
Many faiths and races - the spirit of the place
A multi-cultural way of living that was caring, sharing, giving,
A true community.

Anne Gee

THE DAY CENTRE

We arrive - 'Good morning all,'
And then we take our chairs.
The tea and toast is ready
For anyone who cares.
We smile a little, nod our heads
And ask, 'And how are you?'
Then we take a little walk -
(Mostly to the loo!)

Now - 'What's for dinner?' 'Here's my cash'
The Scrabble counters click.
The card school is in progress
But goodness! Time goes quick!
Before we can believe it
It's home time once again.
The drivers show their great big grins
And tell us we're a pain!

What would we do without them all
Who chivvy us each day?
I think a medal is deserved -
They surely earn their holiday!

Peggy Hemmings

ALL ARE GODS

Choose whoe'er you will to be your Lord
And you be, with them, in full accord,
The king of your soul, enthroned and crowned,
Unknown to the world or else renowned;
It matters not, all are gods.

Perchance a mystic, a seer or sage,
One who is the hero of his age,
A prophet with his teachings divine,
A mighty king of dynastic line;
So be it, all are hallowed.

Your soul may cry out for a goddess,
A Holy Mother, no more nor less,
One who will enrich your body's seed
And make it fruitful, as is your need;
So be it, all are hallowed.

The queen of your soul could be a maid
Who gave her blood on an altar laid;
A goddess of streams and healing wells,
Of love's enchantments and beauty's spells;
So be it, all are hallowed.

Unwilling victims of axe or knife
Both boy-child and youth surrendered life,
Giving all in ritual and rite,
Their deathless souls ascending to Light,
It matters not, all are gods.

Ralph Smith

MR JEKYLL & MRS HIDE

Willingly became his bride
unaware of a darker side
trapped on a roller coaster ride
with a real Jekyll and Hyde.

Just a slap across the cheek
no need to guidance seek
only lost one night's sleep
still a love true and deep.

Accidentally blackens your eye
feel fine after a cry
but beginning to wonder why
and what happened to Mr Shy?

Heavier become the blows
impossible to hide a broken nose
anxiety and desperation grows
possibly your fault you suppose.

Behaviour of a wild boar
x-rays reveal a fractured jaw
definitely the last straw
unable to cope any more.

He is blinded by a red mist
punching with an iron fist
then explanations with a twist
long gone the wedded bliss.

It all ends so ironically
dutifully preparing his tea
decided you're going to flee
his mistress phones 'he is staying with me.'

A C Small

MOMENT

I saw your smile again today,
The stars exploded in the milky way.
The Earth ceased spinning, the tides stood still,
My heart stopped beating of its own free will.
Sunlight filled my frozen mind
Senseless, dumbstruck, breathless, blind.
Ever more my eyes will see
Your beauty framed eternally.

Andrew Hirst

MERCIFUL METICULOUS MAGIC . . .

With a child-like quality she passed through life
caring for others especially in strife
All who knew her she touched with her magic
leaving her mark though often tragic
Her way with children, loving animals dearly
was a God-given gift you could see quite clearly
Precious people pass your way once
To have that privilege, treasure each ounce
she made my life so worthwhile, I have to say
I really am so glad that Morag came my way
Happy she is at peace with her only son
the love of her life and now they are one . . .

Jean Tennent Mitchell

HARVEST FESTIVAL

The children all dressed in their best a basket in their hand,
the choir singing loud and clear the local silver band,
Down the aisle they walked in step up to the altar tall,
each basket then collected and stacked against the wall,
All things bright and beautiful the children then did sing,
lifting up their voices to make the rafters ring,
The service went quite well I thought the children a delight,
no one there could find a fault a really moving sight.

Now with the service over all wandered up to see,
the gifts the children gave today stacked high above the knee,
Boxes of fruit and tins galore all waiting to be sorted,
to give the needy people and other worthwhile causes,
The little boxes looked so nice some bursting out with toys;
they'll go to the local hospital for the girls and boys,
The fruit ones that were given some in disarray,
where children nibbled at the fruit when coming here today.

An apple core was left in one, banana skin another,
so glad the names aren't on each box a shaming for the mother,
But we all laughed, look forward to this yearly sight to see,
for if the boxes stayed intact, disappointed we would be,
As we all left the service a smile on each one's face,
watching the children run about exhausted with their pace,
We all agreed a great success another perfect harvest,
and maybe this year it really was the very, very best.

K Townsley

SNAILS PROTESTING TO MANKIND

We snails are breaking no law
yet, gardeners and farmers hate us so much
We are created to move slow
And go inside our shell at slightest touch!

Why is Man so cruel to us?
We are here for a purpose
We are all part of Creation
Not candidates for extermination!

Man is out to kill us from spring to fall
Trying to get rid of us, once and for all
Green slug pellets give an awful death
I'd rather die in a beer trap!

Some gardeners use broken egg shell
Others put down bark chippings as well
It's not at all nice, that I can tell
Why do we have to go through such Hell?

Though we have no wings we cannot fly
most of us are thrown in next-door's garden
Then thrown back whence they came
without the gardener getting the blame.

There will come a time and mark this well
When a huge drought will hit this land
The French will survive but you . . . will not
Because by then, you will have got rid of us . . .
The lot!

Raymond Spiteri

BOREDOM'S QUAY

Writing doggerel,
rhythm and rhyme
throughout
the monstrousness of time.
Welcome the music
of the spheres
which shows poor truth
in sad arrears.
As timeless as pencil
on plaster . . .
the days can't run
any faster.
As rich as a
roomful of smiles . . .
like a night
out on the tiles?
Tall from sitting
on others' shoulders . . .
small from suffering
proud spite's boulders.
Searching o'er
a seething sea
for ships that scarce
slip boredom's quay.

S Shaw

NATURAL NELSON!

Born by a travellers' caravan in a tent near a quarry of stone
A child was born of travellers' stock a campsite was his home
A midwife helped the child to birth some whiskey was her pay
Nelson Wilson came to life and entered in the day

Travelling life is harsh and tough moving from here to there
In summer 'neath a canvas tent pitched when it was fair
In wintertime they quartered, ensconced in house of stone
Gadgie's seldom welcomed, roon about their home

I remember the first time I met him, forty odd years ago
He chapped on the door of my parents, this man with a natural flow
I played him a song that he fancied the tune had caught his quick ear
He sang me a song in return we both had rapport since that year

He's a gardener to trade for living borders of flowers and grass
His tools of the trade he carts in a van to earn himself ready made cash
He learned as a child by the campsite to utilise things you can see
To fortify body it eases the mind from any old bad tirravie

He gardens and bottles and harvests fruit from the garden of God
Whatever he sees in front of his eyes recycles with Nelson's haud
Relaxing and easy, his singing mellow as home-made old wine
It's pleasant to be in his company he entertains folk a' the time

He flows like the change in the seasons through summer and winter
and fall
And eats what he culls from the garden, then sleeps when the winter
wind calls
A drink of his wine when he's thirsty, it's pressed from the grapes
that he found
Some of his life force aye rubs off on you, when
Natural Nelson's around

Roy A Millar

OUT OF REACH

O' to be free
Like a warm blue sea
Rushing to shores
No boundaries or doors
Out of reach
As on a deserted beach

O' to be free
Flying so high
Like a bird in the sky
No cages to hold
Out of reach
Flying to a favourite niche

O' to be free
Swimming through waves
Like fish in the sea
No tanks or nets
Out of reach
Swimming oceans, not in captivity

Chris Leggett

ON SOLITUDE

Loneliness, come be my friend,
   I cannot bear to see,
A crowd of insincerity,
   Come crowding down on me!

Just being alone is comforting,
   No others must I please;
So loneliness surround me
   And bring me to my knees!

Please loneliness, encompass me,
   Bad company I shun;
For being my own companion,
   I find - is much more fun!

I crave not conversation,
   My interests lie elsewhere;
In dreams I visit deserts,
   And find that no one's there!

My silent admiration,
   Must lie where none have seen;
No one can speak about me,
   They don't know where I've been!

When restless thoughts come calling,
   They plague my vacant heart:
For love and I are thriving,
   Because we are apart!

My wisdom grows with silence,
   I learn each passing day;
Come loneliness surround me,
   And keep them all at bay!

My sustenance is timeless,
  No longer need I food;
For body, mind and spirit,
  Seek only solitude!

R Bissett

IAN'S DAWN CHORUS

He started at dawn, when the birds were on song,
The day has been, hard and long.
Tractor and plough, now still and silent in the field,
The very beginning of autumn's yield.
Turned soil, rich and dark,
Furrows long, and furrows marked.

He enters the pub, for a pint of Special Brew,
No need to look, at the menu.
For he orders a pie, with suet crust,
When it arrives, he eyes it with lust.
He's a man, with a hearty appetite,
Lifting the fork, for his first bite.

As he eats, he reflects on the day,
He's tired and weary, but can't change his ways.
For his love of life, is in the fields and open space,
Given by God, in His grace.
Be it sunshine, or be it rain,
Tomorrow, he'll start with the dawn chorus again.

A Jones

THE COUNTRYSIDE

As fields we pass where rivers flow,
On yonder hill where forests grow,
Cows, sheep and rabbits too,
When in the country come in to view.

Cottages with ivy growing,
Roses bloom and apple blossoms,
Barking dogs at garden gate,
Church getting ready for the summer fete

The smell of the country makes you heady,
In fields the corn is ripe and ready,
Fruit on the trees is ready to drop,
Pears, plums and apples, what a crop.
A farmer's work is never done, from early morn
                                        to the evening sun.

Wendy Walker

I STAND GUARD

Faithfully I sat, on that green mat
Guarding treasures gladly
While occupants trekked far and wide
Searching shores and cliffs on t'other side.
Oceans, craggs, cliffs and great waters
Tales of ventures, loss of sons and daughters
Adventures of its peoples from this and distant shores.

My mind had strayed a moment or two
Not minding passers by, nor what I was left to do
Silently I thumbed the mental book and paused as I viewed each page
Thinking of what villagers did in this and far off age
Excitement gripped me as I looked into the portals of my mind
Within my reach there was that captain bold and brave
To his men he shouted loudly, 'Aye, aye, me hearties!
Let's get this cargo shifted soon, let's clear the decks, me hearties!'

Before the dream became reality, me dears,
A shout rang loud and clear, 'Look what I've brought you Gran!'
Up I got and struggled on, to inspect the latest treasure,
My biggest bubble burst and I was back in Morecambe.
Had I stayed a moment more, I would be gone forever
On that lovely metal trail of piracy and leisure.

A C Yap-Morris

THE SHADOW

Creaking floors
wind blowing through
the curtains stand
very tall

Dark figurines
give us a fright
ghostly presence
are in sight

Is it a shadow
that's walking by
the closed window?
Oh my!

Kristina Howells

THE LAST BRITISH HOVERCRAFT

As I passed the hovercraft terminal
On Southsea seafront, I stopped for a spell
To watch the hovercraft sail up the shore
As I have done so many times before.
Just ten minutes later it sailed away
Looking spectacular amidst the spray,
To watch - a small crowd always gathers here,
We sailed on it again only last year
To re-visit Ryde on the Isle of Wight
On a calm, crisp winter's day, clear and bright.
It's the last hovercraft in the country,
The only other one was nice to see
Five years ago at Dover, now it's gone,
Now ours at Southsea is the only one.
Invented by Christopher Cockerell,
A unique popular vessel made well,
In those days a nice new form of transport,
All round the world they are being much sought,
There's a museum at Lee-on-Solent,
If I go I know I'll be glad I went,
They've got hovercraft ancient and modern,
I reckon there will be a lot to learn,
From home I take a half-hour walk some days
To see Britain's last hovercraft. I gaze
Across the Solent to Ryde beach and spy
The craft through my binoculars, I try
To focus. The eight minute sail is nice
From Southsea to an island paradise.

Gill Coombes

BULLIES

'Specky little four-eyes!' That's what they'd say
A new insult I'd have to handle each day
Didn't want to go to school when I awoke,
Knowing when I did, fun at me they'd poke!
They knew there was no way that I'd complain
Or the punishment I received would start over again.

My best friend (Jamaica Jim) suffered just like me,
The colour of his skin made his life a misery,
Very trying, often crying, constantly on guard
As bullies chased us all around that old school yard.
No place to hide, no refuge could we seek,
Nothing else to do but turn the other cheek.

Little Mary Brown had a defect in one eye,
They would creep up on her blind side - scare her till she cried!
Like me, she couldn't understand their threats and their demands,
Orders of money to be given on command,
Hurtful messages during lessons they would send,
Each evening I'd ask the Lord for the night to never end!

Karl Jakobsen

HERON DYKE

In the late 1930s,
Not yet in my teens,
I used to go fishing
In the Somerset rheens.

It was a good day for fishing, to go fishing for pike
And I was determined to try Heron Dyke.
Where the bullrushes swayed to the soft western breeze
And I could sit sheltered 'neath the old willow trees
And watch the kingfishers on blue-spangled wings
Dash past to their nest by the old cattle rings
Where they'd made a home in a hole in the bank,
Just half a hand's breadth 'neath the old water tank,
Half-hidden behind the bullrushes' clump,
Undeterred by the clank of the old water pump,
Where they'd stab at the water with poniard-like beaks
And take to their young 'uns the bright silver bleak.

But big pike were in there, down in the green weeds,
With gurt jaws a-grinnin' and eyes like stone beads.
Oh, they lay in ambush in water's cold sheath,
With gurt jaws hair-triggered and a hundred sharp teeth.
Oh, big fish were in there, of that I was sure
And knowing the water I thought I might lure
A fish or three.
Maybe four.
Perhaps even five!
(For as all fishermen know, in matters piscernal,
A good swim of water makes hope leap eternal.)
Oh-ah . . . doesn't it just!

John Whittock

THIS GARDEN OF MINE

There's a handful of memories in this
Garden of mine,
'Yet we can't see the wood for the trees'.

There's notches been made where a
Family have grown,
Yet we've covered them up with the leaves.

There's flowers still struggling to
Come out and survive,
Given from friends of the past,
The flowers still bloom in a dried up earth,
Yet the friendships don't always last.

A book could be written in this garden of mine
And the pages turned over like leaves
And we'd find the reason for the mistakes
We have made,
'We can't see the wood for the trees'.

June Sedgebear

THE NIGHT THE CAUSEWAY COLLAPSED

The wind was fierce, the waves were high,
The night was dark and grim.
No soul was seen, no soul was heard,
The light subdued and dim.

Then through the night a muffled sound,
Of maroon first once then twice.
It struck the hearts of all inside
Eight men responded in a trice.

'Twas useless as they ran to save,
They could only stare, they knew.
For the Strood, the only island road
Had vanished, before eyes of lifeboat crew.

Whatever disaster fell that night
Must wait until the morn.
No way to transport, nowhere to go.
So many to die, no one to know.

The lines were down, the water up,
As surge after surge from northern sea,
Battered the houses and sunk the boats,
Shriek after shriek - God, please help me.

Seven thousand souls were drowned that night,
They had nowhere to go.
The land itself began to shake as it was torn apart
No one to see or mourn as the island lost its heart

No island now off Anglia shore,
But layers of sea, shining bright.
No sound was heard, no soul was seen,
The end of a dreadful night.

J L A Grinham

A POP STAR'S LIFE

Hard work and talent to be in the game
Fame and fortune is their aim
Travelling far, no fixed abode
Always being in singing mode.

Climb through the ranks to number one
You're at the top it's just begun
Parties, friends, who do you trust
Is it love or is it lust?

No privacy, someone's always there
All around you, people stare
Always chased, you run and hide
Place of safety, home inside.

Lots of money to buy what you choose
A house, a car, lots of booze
A wife, a family, who can tell
You could end up in a living hell.

Public acclaim, you worry a bit
You're only as good as your next hit
The press, they follow, wherever you go
You have no secrets, they don't know.

Shuttered windows, at home with the wife
Do you like your pop star's life?
A roof, a floor, four walls, locked door
Anonymity, need I say more.

Dale Finlay

THE TRAIN

There's a brick made train on a brick made track
It can't move forward and it won't move back.
You won't hear the wheels go clickety-clack
Thundering down the railroad track.
There is no driver on this train
No fireman to shovel coal again and again.
You won't hear the whistle sounding some mournful cry
No smoke belching into the midnight sky.
A monument of bygone times
A tribute to happier times.
When steam trains they reigned supreme
Along came Beeching and shattered their dreams.
Steam trains confined to the breakers' yards
Workers simply got their cards.
Workshops it seems were needed no more
Thousands of people were shown the door.
Tracks torn up and stations closed down
Beeching did this with many a frown.
For when you see the brick made train
Think on, you won't see its like again.
To the man who thought this scheme
Thanks, you have made my boyhood dream.

Jack Iddon

MY PERFECT ROSE

You are my rose
You are my love
You are my tender little white dove
You make me happy
You make me smile
My feelings run so deep
It makes it hard for me to sleep
I really need you by my side
One day I hope you'll be my bride.

Graham Cooke

MATT AND ELISA

Matt and Elisa are on the radio
They are on every morning
So why not, let's go
And listen to the show
Between 6 and 10am
So we make sure to listen to them

For they are the ultimate
Bird and bloke
Who can have
A laugh and a joke

And if you can guess the
Brain teaser you will get a mention
From Matt and Elisa
And if you guess the right year
You will get a big cheer.

Coleen Bradshaw

JUST SIXTY-THREE

Love makes the world go round you can bet on that
Yes my love and by golly that's a fact
What memories darling as in the years gone by
My old mind goes back to when we first met I sigh
It was I that was told that a young lass you see
Fancied me. Found out it was so true just little me
Well love I was to put it to the test that's so
We had finished work at Brentford Palm Toffee Factory
'Would you go to the pictures (films)?' you replied, 'No.'
Well I did but try thought they were having a joke with me
But on the next day you asked me if I meant to give you an answer
I do not say what I do not mean, no fear
To prove same asked you to come with me that night.
'Yes,' you replied, my heart went bomp tiddly bomp.
Good cheer, was that love? It must have been make that clear.

J Sexton

BOWLS, BOWLS, BOWLS

We three ladies of bowling prowess
Love our bowls as you may well guess
We roll them up and roll them back
And hope that we get near the jack.

Oddfellows is the name by which we're known
We play far away and we play at home
We play every day if the weather allows
We wear grey skirts and a lovely white blouse.

Our bums might be big and our legs might be short
But our husbands love us and give us support
Though if a choice was made between bowling and him
We'd have to admit the bowling would win.

Gill Casey

MY OWN AMBITION

I remember the bright dreams that
faded so dull,
I remember the doubters taking
their toll,
I remember the wishing night after
night,
That just one day I'll win the
fight,
I remember thinking my life needed
to change,
And believing for the better to
stop the pain,
The ambition so strong I couldn't
deny,
The talent seemed absent gone
awry,
I remember the tears of solitary
pain,
Being alone wanting so badly to
gain,
The dreams are still alive burning
bright in the sky,
The dreams to deliver that were
always too high.

Nicholas Pearce

IF FATHER HADN'T DIED

If father hadn't died, this tale I could not tell
For he had provided, this I remember well
I was just eleven, the baby only two,
Mam was left to raise us, the poor house helped us through.

Our home it was a holding, sparsely to provide,
How was Mam to manage
With no Father by her side.

It seemed there was no way out
With seven mouths to feed
Clogs, clothes for the school wear
And all the things we need.

My path, it was stony, too much for me to bear
I had to be a mother, with tiny tots to share.

Somehow we did manage, with Mam away outside
Me inside the kitchen, the children by my side.

Time had passed so quickly, the years had passed me by
My future loomed before me, it was time to say goodbye.

Mam she did marry, for the children a brand-new dad
He took on the holding, left us feeling sad.

It was then I met my true love, by the church on Sunday night
We kissed, he proposed to marry and all the world looked bright.

Seeds of marriage nurtured, with four children of my own,
So different from the childhood, that myself had known.

The clock moves on, the pendulum swings
Oh how the time does fly
I am back beside the holding, I wake up with a sigh.

Today I am a great-great-grandma, have lost my girlish pride
Would my life have been different
If Father hadn't died?

Daisy Cooper

LUCY THE LOUSE

Lucy was head louse
Who lived in lots of hair
Curly, straight, short and long,
She didn't really care.

She crawled up past the temples
And settled in the fringe
She slept a while and then awoke
All set to have a binge.

She loved the juicy food she found
Just beneath the skin
She bit and tasted warm, red blood
And really sucked it in.

When feet grew itchy she moved on
Now hunger was at bay
She then had lots of work to do
With many eggs to lay.

She dotted many shafts of hair
With nits of white and brown
Then she met her many friends
To crawl both up and down.

Her enemies were fingernails
Which often scratched around
Or small tooth combs which came her way
To knock her to the ground.

But she was strong and she survived
Till lotion gave her pain
It soaked, then suffocated
And flushed her down the drain!

G Peat

IN THE LAND OF . . .

In the land of spiky haircuts
All the fellows look alike
And there's thousands 'murder' pop songs
If they can swallow down a mike!

In the land of big-boob-girl-bands
None play instruments at all
But they wiggle most delightful
When they sing 'Yeah Baby Doll!'

In the land of baldy-head-shaves
Male and female look the same
And it's really most confusing
Should one try a 'blind-date-game!'

In the land of music moguls
Albums, discs and singles rank . . .
(By some 'spiky', 'boobs' or 'baldies')
Just like 'money-in-the-bank'!

But in the land of 'Rip-Van-Winkles'
Where the OAPs abide
'Spikes' and 'boobs' and 'unshaved-baldies'
Have *gone out with the tide!*

Bob Mackay

A CARING MOTHER

Mother sitting in her old armchair
Someone who had many a care
Her tired body worn out and thin
But the twinkle in her eyes could never be dimmed.

She had brought up her family without any aid
Taking in washing for little pay
Scrubbing and cleaning from morning till night
For the love of her family she would put up a fight.

Father would come home from his shift at the pit
Out came the tin bath in which he would sit
Mother would scrub him to get rid of the dust
And then do his washing, this was a must.

Life was hard but with mother there
The family survived with her great care.

Audrey Machon Grayson

MAY DAY

From the moment we are born we are dying
There's no need for you to be crying
Many things out there to be done
Before the last setting of the sun . . .

Places to see for us to cherish
People to meet before we perish
Answers to be found which were once lost
Our first ice age was a thick frost
We all have things that we must learn
Before Earth crashes and we all burn
Let's all get started on our missions
Release your closed mind from its prison.

Time is ticking by at a quick pace
Mass destruction of the human race
Have you figured out what you are here for
To live your life by universal law
Animals are hurting and so am I
Unity is waiting please you must try
Peace and love is all around you
Believe in love and it will guide you . . .

From the moment we are born we are dying
There's no need for you to be crying
Many things out there to be done
Before the last setting of the sun
Before the last setting of the sun.

Kerri Morehu-Baker

HERS AND HIS

When he has gone, though sad and though blue
I'll do all those things I have wanted to do!
I'll sing and play music; I'll wear what I like!
Won't cook, clean or shop but read books and just flop!
I'll decorate the house but first hold a rave
I'll send to the charities all naff presents he gave!
I'll hang up the pictures I bought at boot sales
And ignore all those people saying, 'She's off the rails!'
I'll dump his mum's furniture and buy from Ikea
And do OU study on war and Crimea.
But it was so silly to leave poems around
And he finished it on the day it was found.
Now she has gone I watch TV and sport!
I go to the cake shop for what she never bought!
I buy 'trashy' tabloids for page three and the scandal!
I don't do the garden - she'd call me a vandal!
I've thrown the naff jumpers she knitted for me
And all those food items that were buy, get one free!
I go to the pub and come back *really* late
I've wangled some help for the jobs that I hate!
I've dumped all the ornaments bought at boot sales
Found room for my shirts on the wardrobe rails!
But who was to blame for not heeding signs?
Perhaps they, like you, should have read 'tween the lines!

Di Castle

SECRET LOVE

Imagination is where I can see,
The most beautiful things, that means something to me.
I am happy, you can see that I smile,
But when I am sad, I haven't seen you for a while.
That wonderful scent, is what I miss,
Your eyes, your face, I long for your kiss.
Dreaming of you all night long,
Blood pumping fast, heart beating strong.
Thinking of you from morning till eve,
Brain in a trance, hard to breathe.
Courage is what I'm trying to find,
To ask you to dinner, in my fragile mind.
All the seasons, year after year,
Talking to you my heart sheds a tear.
Wishing each day you could be mine,
Only your love is sweeter than wine.
No one knows about the way I feel,
Fantasy or illusion I know that you're real.

Ray Stuart

A RIDE

The monkey and the elephant
Went for a ride on a camel's back.
The monkey slipped off
Because the elephant coughed
And the elephant laughed till he cried.
The camel said, 'That's the last time
I take you for a ride.'

I Jerome

FANTASY
YEAH, RIGHT

I see a rainbow long and bright,
At the end a glowing light.
Look at the light, what do you see?
A pot of gold, for you and me.

At the bottom of my garden, among the lilies,
A bunch of friendly flower fairies.
A special friend of mine - Angelina, dressed in pink,
Tells me of a magical five-legged cat called Skink.

I find the cat, I can't see,
The extra leg there's meant to be.
She can't speak either, so I can see,
It's all in my head - *imaginary!*

Rachael Tennant (13)

GILFACH GOCH

I was born in Gilfach Goch, eleven Fountain Row
My father was a miner, who worked the earth below

Its stream was my swimming pool, its trees were my swings
On cardboard I'd slide down its mountainside on wings

Our mother would go scrubbing other people's floors
Just to make our Christmas special and to buy us all new clothes

I was born one of six, three sisters and two brothers
And I could not have wished, for a better dad or mother

We had no fancy kitchen, with all the new mod cons
Just a pantry underneath the stairs, where no light ever shone

We had a toilet out the back, that I did not want to use
Instead of nice soft Andrex, we had strips of daily news

No bathroom with a shower, just a tin bath on the wall
That was placed before the fire, and used to bath us all

No nice soft carpets at our feet, we had flagstones cold and hard
But we did have nice coal fires, surrounded by a guard

We never had hot water bottles to keep us warm in bed
We had bricks from out the oven, wrapped up in sheets instead.

Allan Gordon Pengelly

BIG BOAB

Big Boab they say was a man of the land
Everyone else's close at hand
Be it sheep, tatties or even a hare
In the grey dark, Boab wid be down for a share
But then he took ill an' it wisnae very kind
An' the big man just said, 'Ach ah dinnae mind.'
At the end he told us, 'Am in an awfy bad way.'
He fought hell for six years, what more can I say?

Thomas McAdam

THINGS I DIDN'T SAY

I didn't say I love
As often as I should.
If you were with me now my dear
I would feel so good.

If I could just see you
Just for one more day,
I would spend it telling you
All the things I didn't say.

Things like how proud I was
To be your loving wife,
How happy you made me feel
Through 35 years of married life.

I'd thank you for our 3 children
That we had together,
How we got through life
When there was stormy weather.

How brave you were when
The big C ravaged your brain,
It happened so quickly
Life was never the same.

On that September night
Unconscious in bed you lay.
I just held your hand
Without a word to say.

I didn't say I love you
And how much I really cared.
To thank you for the happiness
In life that we both shared.

All too soon God smiled down on you
All your suffering gone,
With you my love so true
My husband for so long.

4 years down the road
I think of you each day.
I regret and feel remorseful
For the things I didn't say.

Yvonne Lewis

DO YOU KNOW ROSS-ON-WYE?

Do you know Ross? The town of Ross-on-Wye
Redolent with history from the days gone by.
Elegant upon her hill she stands
In beauty fashioned long ago by skilful hands.
The massive market house crowns the long climb,
Built of huge sandstone blocks rough-kissed by time.
St Mary's needle spire stands sharp against the sky
High on the cliff above the river and the fields that round her lie.
Though parking needs have ripped away old corners full of charm
The shape of secret lanes lives on to hide the harm.
From prospect point one sees the river, swift and wide,
A silver path across the countryside.
John Kyrle, the benefactor of the town,
In spirit and in effigy looks down
Upon the weekly market gathered for the trade
That's flourished busily since the small town was made.
And winter's rage could swell the Wye and flood the plain
Leaving the whole town dry to look down in disdain.
Then the town stretched to levels where the angry floods encroach
And swamp the buildings at the town's approach.
But hilltop Ross laughs at needless, self-inflicted pain
As it stands secure, untouched by flood in spite of heavy rain.
Ross has a comfortable air of yesterday
That speaks of restfulness in an engaging way.
The town has its mystery, secret but sublime,
Born of its history and honed by time.

Flora Hughes

THE ART GALLERY

It all began when my son-in-law
Hung some pictures for us on the wall,
Commenting, 'You'll have to get some more
For your art gallery in the hall.'

And from then on the seed was planted;
My husband began his collection,
Till soon the walls were supplanted
With pictures, hardly one empty section.

He's added to them as he's got older;
No masterpieces, none stands alone.
Beauty's in the eye of the beholder;
Who cares if their names are unknown?

Antique and charity shops he must visit
On our excursions up into town.
He just doesn't have the will to resist
In his search for a picture of renown.

But we're fast running out of wall space.
He'll part with none to make way for new;
We'll soon have to move to a bigger place,
In other words, to a different view!

Marlene Allen

THE GLORY OF THE CHASE
(A MERRY DANCE)

Old Reynard is a splendid fellow, in coat of reddish-brown
Who holds himself in high regard, on account of his renown.

The sly and sneaky, scheming cove maintains a devious campaign
To improve his roguish image and redeem his sullied name.

Traditionally a country dweller, he preyed upon the plenty
Plundered from the large estates of hunting, shooting gentry.

The country squires were not amused, by the twister's crafty grin.
With horse and hound and hunting horn, they sought to do him in.

Their quarry was not minded to fight them, toe to toe,
Instead, by stealth and subterfuge, he'd oft' evade his foe.

But flight is short-termism, so the knave evolved a cunning scheme
To persuade we, *Homo Sapiens*, that he really isn't mean.

Thus, in the daylight hours, he grins and looks real cute
And delays, for darkness cover, his murderous pursuits.

City folk, all now convinced of the shyster's true docility,
The right to hunt they seek to ban, from now until eternity.

The issue's gone, for arbitration, to the highest in the land,
Whilst 'Slyboots', unmolested, laughs at us behind his hand.

And so, in time of crisis, while England's going down the pan,
MPs sit round, debating, whether foxes can be chased, by man.

Gary Pike

THE VISITORS

I was once diving on the sea bed,
in the distance were lights glowing red.
What they were I could not say
because they were too far away.
They divided and became more
then rose from the ocean floor.
They broke the surface and seemed to fly
lifting into the sky.
They darted about in a random weave
what they were I cannot perceive.
We watched them for many hours
through rain and showers.
But it was now time to leave this place
if we were to avoid the tidal race.
Just then they joined as one,
in the blink of an eye they were gone.
They left colours, red, blue and a strange green
also trails ultra violet where they had been.

S Glover

FANTASY STEAMTOWN

The Steamtown lad is called Michael,
He goes to work on his motorcycle,
Michael polishes the engines and makes them shine,
He moved to Carnforth from Newcastle-upon-Tyne.

Michael will soon be seventeen,
He works hard to keep the carriages clean,
They are the type that have narrow corridors,
And small compartments with sliding doors,
He cleans the outer windows, then does them inside,
Ready for the tourists when they go on their ride.

One of the staff is old Mark Tate,
He sits in his office near the main gate,
Mark greets the tourists with a cheerful smile,
As they pay him and go through the turnstile.

The 1306 Mayflower steam engine is on the track,
It travels from Carnforth to York City and back,
You can visit The National Railway Museum
And explore the city,
To miss this opportunity would surely be a great pity.

The engine driver is Matthew Ford,
He shouts to the passengers, 'All aboard!'
Michael stands on the platform,
In his railwayman's uniform,
He walks alongside the carriages looking very smart,
Then he blows his whistle for the train to start,
A large cloud of steam belches out from the funnel,
As the train moves off and out through the tunnel.

When they return from their day trip,
Some of the tourists give Michael a tip,
A few of them come from overseas,
There are Americans, Germans and sometimes Japanese,
Michael says he likes the job although his wages are poor,
But the tips he receives help to make it a little bit more.

Dave Birkinshaw

AN OBSERVER OF RULES

An observer of rules is a dignified man
He wears a bow tie and carries a pen,
He'll keep to the limit when driving along
And never does anything dreadfully wrong.

An observer of rules will not overtake
He will hold up the traffic to keep it sedate,
He will not ignore an important road sign
Or lose concentration thus risking a fine.

An observer of rules will pay his poll tax
And always cover the blade of his axe,
He makes rigidly sure of his facts in advance
And never leaves something remotely to chance.

An observer of rules is a stickler for time
And will always queue in an orderly line,
He will not arrive for a rendezvous late
Or dream of upsetting a socialist date.

An observer of rules will fill in his forms
Water his plants and mow his lawns,
He will always be a reliable friend
And keep to his rule book right up to the end.

Elizabeth Cleveland

TELEVISIONS

It tells you the crime and it tells you the news
but some things you have to refuse
like the bad things that harm you
and if you watch too much of it that's what you'll want to do.
It might weigh a tonne
you might've guessed it's a television
it shows you the world and things you haven't seen
but some shows are bad and make you mean
it tells you the news and tells you the crime
but some shows are stupid and are wasting your time.

Sylvester Espana